World War II
Pacific

by
Walter A. Hazen

CE National, Inc.
1003 Presidential Dr.
P. O. Box 365
Winona Lake, IN 46590

Cover Graphics by
Vickie Lane

Inside Illustrations by
Pat Biggs

Cover Photo
UPI/Corbis-Bettmann

Publisher
Instructional Fair • TS Denison
Grand Rapids, Michigan 49544

Permission to Reproduce

About the Author

Walter A. Hazen received his Bachelor of Science in Education from Troy State University. He also holds a master's degree from the University of Tennessee, where he majored in deaf education. A secondary history teacher with over 30 years of experience, Walter spent the last several years of his career teaching and developing curriculum for deaf students.

Credits

Author: Walter A. Hazen
Cover Graphics: Vickie Lane
Inside Illustrations: Pat Biggs
Project Director/Editor: Sharon Kirkwood
Editors: Lisa Hancock, Rhonda DeWaard
Production: Pat Geasler, Vickie Lane

Photos: Corbis–Bettman
UPI/Corbis–Bettmann
Reuters/Corbis–Bettmann

Standard Book Number: 1-56822-452-4
World War II–Pacific
Copyright © 1997 by Instructional Fair • TS Denison
2400 Turner Avenue NW
Grand Rapids, Michigan 49544
All Rights Reserved • Printed in the USA

Table of Contents

In the 1930s, the militaristic government of Japan announced a foreign policy it called "The Greater East Asia Co-Prosperity Sphere." It was a policy designed to bring all of Asia and the Pacific islands under the influence and control of Japan. At first, this ambitious and aggressive plan appealed to some Asians, even in the Philippines where the United States had held sway since the Spanish-American War. After all, some Asians reasoned, the Japanese were racially akin to themselves, and any economic empire controlled by Asians at the exclusion of Westerners was appealing. It took only a short period of brutal Japanese rule, however, to make those Asians realize how wrong their assessment of the Japanese had been.

Japanese aggression in Asia and the Pacific eventually led to conflict with the United States. When the American government ceased selling vital war-related materials to Japan in the summer of 1941, the militarists in control there knew war with the U.S. was inevitable. This realization led to the infamous attack on Pearl Harbor on December 7, 1941.

World War II in the Pacific differed from the war in Europe in a number of ways. First, the enemy in the Pacific was a fanatical foe who put honor and death in combat above everything else, and whose emperor promoted the view that other peoples are barbarians fit only for subjugation. Second, the fighting took place over a vast area, the battlefield ranging throughout Asia and across most of the Pacific Ocean. And third, the Pacific war was a struggle dominated by carrier-based aircraft. There were naval battles fought in which opposing ships fired few shots; in one case, no shots were fired at all. Most of the fighting at sea was carried out by airplanes.

Sources vary, but some say as many as 50 million died in World War II, with 17 million of these deaths having occurred in Asia and in the Pacific. This statistic attests to the tenacity of the fighting in those areas.

The Eye on History series strives to bring history to life through the personal experiences of those who lived them. The letters, postcards, diary accounts, and so on are fictitious. However, the facts contained in them represent what individuals might have written. The more students are able to experience history through what others may have felt and thought, the more meaningful it will be. After all, history is not just musty dates and facts. History is the stories of individuals and nations and of heroes and ordinary people. It is influenced by fashions and passions. We hope this series will help students understand history in new and exciting ways.

Special Bulletin

The American Embassy, Tokyo
March 3, 1936

More assassinations have taken place over the last few days. One of the first people to be killed was Finance Minister Takahashi, who had vigorously opposed the Japanese army's request for additional military spending. Any Japanese politician who refuses to bow down to the militarists is in jeopardy of losing his life.

It is apparent that the militarists are now in strong control of the government. They have convinced the Japanese people that the conquest of Manchuria was justified and necessary. They pointed out that Japan's population had more than doubled in 60 years and the nation needed more land because it was incapable of feeding its people. They also pointed to the vast coal and oil deposits of Manchuria — resources that the empire needed to become a world power. Not the least of their propaganda ploys was their assertion that the Japanese are a superior people and destined to control all of Asia.

The Japanese got away with it in Manchuria. They received only a slap on the wrist from the League of Nations. Will they get away with it the next time?

The seeds for World War II in the Pacific were planted in September of 1931, when Japan seized Manchuria. Thus, eight full years before Nazi Germany attacked Poland and started the war in Europe, fighting was already taking place in Asia. Japan followed up her aggression in Manchuria with an invasion of China in 1937.

The world paid little attention as Japan drifted toward a military dictatorship in the1930s. Most nations were too preoccupied with a worldwide depression to be concerned with what the Japanese were doing. Even when Japan invaded Manchuria, she received nothing more than a warning from the League of Nations. It is not surprising that the Japanese viewed this inaction by the free world as a sign of weakness.

The United States was not a member of the League of Nations. It also took no action at the time against the Japanese. No nation wanted to risk starting another world war.

Discuss . . .

- why, considering the cultural differences among the parties involved, Japan would sign a pact with Germany and Italy in 1936 and become one of the Axis Powers.

- whether Nazi Germany and Imperial Japan would have come to blows if either had succeeded in its long-range military plans.

- whether a military dictatorship could ever take over the government of the United States. Explain why or why not.

- whether any people or culture is superior to others. Explain why or why not.

For Further Research

The League of Nations could not stop Japanese aggression in the 1930s. Could the United Nations that was established after World War II have done so? Compare the powers of the two peace-keeping organizations.

Hickam Field, Pearl Harbor, Hawaii
December 8, 1941

Dear Fran,

How do I feel? Shocked. Stunned. Sad. Angry. Yes, more than anything—angry. I felt so helpless not being able to do anything.

We arrived over Pearl at the height of the attack and had no idea what was happening. No one did. Fires were everywhere and things were blowing up all over the place. Many Japanese planes were diving and attacking the ships at the naval base. Others were bombing and strafing the planes at Hickam and Wheeler Fields. I saw fighter planes swoop down low and machine-gun civilians running for cover. And there was nothing I could do to help! Since we were on our way from California, our armor and ammunition had been removed to make room for extra fuel tanks.

I was in a flight of B-17s. Nine of us managed to land at Hickam and run to safety. The other three landed wherever they could, one on a golf course. Several planes were destroyed, but our losses pale in comparison to what happened to the ships in the harbor and the planes on the airstrips. I don't know how many people are dead, but I know the number must be staggering.

Life is so strange. Two days ago I left San Francisco without a care in the world. Now everything is turned upside down.

Don't worry about me. I'll be fine. Say hello to your mom and dad and to that tow-headed little brother of yours. Write as often as you can.

Love,
Jerry

On the morning of December 7, 1941, Japanese planes from aircraft carriers in the Pacific, 200 miles off the island of Oahu, attacked the American naval base and adjacent airfields at Pearl Harbor, Hawaii. The attack came without warning. At the time, most Americans at Pearl Harbor were either in bed, eating breakfast, or preparing to go to church services. Although a radar truck stationed on a nearby hill had picked up blips on its screen indicating the approach of a large number of aircraft, it was assumed that these were the twelve B-17 bombers arriving from California. No action was taken and no alarm was sounded.

The first wave of 183 enemy planes arrived over the islands at approximately 7:55 A.M. A second wave of 175 planes appeared about an hour later. Their main targets were the seven battleships lined up neatly in a row in the harbor. Facing virtually no opposition, Japanese pilots sank three of the large ships and badly damaged the other five. It was fortunate for the United States that the aircraft carriers *Lexington* and *Enterprise* were not in port. Their destruction would have rendered the Pacific fleet useless as a fighting force.

Continued on page 7.

Continued from page 6.

When the attack ended, the United States counted its losses. Almost 3,700 Americans were dead, and more than 1,200 were wounded. Twenty-one ships were sunk or damaged, and more than 300 planes on the ground were destroyed. The following day, December 8, President Franklin D. Roosevelt asked Congress for a declaration of war against Japan.

The Japanese made two crucial mistakes at Pearl Harbor. First, they did not destroy the ship repair facilities at the base. Consequently, most of the ships that were damaged were soon back in action. Second, and more important, they did not seek out and destroy the *Lexington* and the *Enterprise*. Six months later, these very carriers helped deal Japan its first major defeat at the Battle of Midway.

The Japanese attacked Pearl Harbor because the United States was the only obstacle in their path toward the conquest of Asia. They knew they had to destroy the U.S. Pacific fleet if their plans were to succeed. It is frightening how close they came to accomplishing that feat.

Discuss . . .

- what might have happened if the Japanese had followed up their attack on Pearl Harbor with a land invasion of the Hawaiian Islands.
- what would have been the effect on American naval power if the Japanese had located and sunk both the *Lexington* and the *Enterprise*.
- the credibility of the assertion below, and whether you think an American president would have deliberately sacrificed several thousand lives to attain such ends.

  A few students of history maintain that President Roosevelt knew of the impending Japanese attack on Pearl Harbor but did nothing to prevent it. They argue that Roosevelt's inaction stemmed from his desire to bring America into the war on the side of Great Britain. They also point out that Roosevelt believed that increased war production would provide a much-needed boost to the American economy.

Journal Entry
Rangoon, Burma
December 9, 1941

Our Tomahawk fighting planes have finally arrived, and we are anxious to settle some scores—not just for us because of Pearl Harbor, but also for the Chinese. Since 1937, the Japanese have bombed Chinese cities at will. They have killed tens of thousands of innocent civilians and spread terror everywhere. With no Chinese Air Force (so to speak) to oppose them, every bombing raid has been hardly more dangerous than a turkey shoot for the boastful Japanese pilots. I hope that, in protecting the Burma Road, we can make life a little more uncomfortable for them.

Yesterday, after the arrival of our planes, Colonel Chennault briefed us on what to expect in aerial combat with the Japanese. He reminded us again that the Japanese Zero can climb faster than our Tomahawk, and, if we are not careful, we will find ourselves outmaneuvered and shot down. But he also pointed out that our Tomahawk has several decided advantages. It can dive faster and fly faster on the straightaway. More importantly, the Tomahawk is sturdier and better armored. In contrast, the Zero has no armor at all. Hit it in the gas tank and it will explode in a ball of fire.

Even before the Tokyo raid, a small number of American fliers were scoring victories over the Japanese in the skies over Burma and China. These fliers were part of a volunteer group known as the Flying Tigers.

The Flying Tigers arrived in Rangoon, Burma, in September, 1941. Their mission was to protect the Burma Road, a tortuous route that wound its way some 700 miles through mountainous terrain from Lashio, Burma, to Kunming, China. The road was China's lifeline. Because the Japanese sank all ships attempting to supply China by sea, the road was the only way to ensure that the Chinese army received the aid it needed to continue its war against Japan.

The Flying Tigers, whose real name was the American Volunteer Group, or AVG, was formed in the summer of 1941. Pilots came from naval air training stations and army air bases throughout the United States. Of the original 80 pilots who volunteered, half were U.S. Navy flyers. A handful came from the U.S. Marine Flying Corps, and the rest were recruited from the U.S. Army Air Force. The pilots signed one-year contracts to fly for the air force of Chinese leader Generalissimo Chiang Kai-shek. Each pilot was to receive $600 a month, plus a bonus of $500 for each Japanese plane he could prove he destroyed. Flight leaders and squadron leaders were to receive slightly more.

Continued on page 9.

Continued from page 8.

The commander of the Flying Tigers was Colonel (later Brigadier General) Claire Chennault, a retired army captain who jumped at the chance to get back into action. Colonel Chennault had been a high school principal in Louisiana when he joined the U.S. Army Air Service during WWI. He was forced to retire in 1937 because of partial deafness. It was his advocacy of using fast fighter planes to battle bombers in the air that caught the attention of Chiang Kai-shek.

Although the American Volunteer Group was in action for only seven months, it made the most of its brief service. Its first encounter with the enemy came shortly before Christmas in 1941. On December 20, a group of ten Japanese bombers were detected approaching the city of Kunming. The bombers were flying at an arrogantly low altitude, the pilots knowing they had nothing to fear from the Chinese. But to their surprise, they were intercepted by fifteen Flying Tigers who had taken off from their newly constructed airbase near Kunming. The Japanese were no match for this surprise defense. Six of the Japanese bombers were immediately sent spiraling to the earth in flames, while the other four were hit and crashed elsewhere. For a few short months, Japanese air dominance over the Burma Road had ended.

By the time the Flying Tigers were incorporated into the U.S. Army Air Corps in July 1942, AVG pilots had shot down about 300 Japanese planes. Hundreds more that could not be confirmed were probably destroyed. The Flying Tigers' accomplishments were even more remarkable when the number of planes normally at their disposal is taken into account. At no time, because of the scarcity of parts, could the AVG put more than 55 planes in the air at once. But with those 55, they kept the Burma Road open and China in the war.

Discuss . . .

- whether the members of the Flying Tigers were mercenaries in the true sense.
- the reasons why a person might volunteer for a group such as the Flying Tigers.
- what the effect might have been if Japan had conquered all of China.

For Further Study

Find out why the Flying Tigers painted the fierce snout of a tiger shark on the noses of their planes.

LUZON

CABANATUAN

BATAAN
PENINSULA

MANILA

CORREGIDOR

Journal Entry
Corregidor
May 3, 1942

Will this rocky island in Manila Bay be the last land I see? We cannot hold out much longer. The Japanese have bombed and shelled us for twenty-seven straight days. Supplies and ammunition are deplorably low, and the number of sick and wounded mount every day. We are facing starvation, and many of us suffer from malaria.

General Wainwright has been placed in a difficult position. He knows that if Corregidor doesn't surrender soon, the Japanese will likely slaughter everyone taking refuge in the tunnel. This number includes more than 1,200 Filipino civilians and over 60 American nurses. On the other hand, the commander of the Japanese forces, General Yamashita, insists that General Wainwright order other fighting units throughout the islands to surrender at the same time. Yamashita vows he will kill every prisoner in his charge if General Wainwright does not comply. It seems certain that the general will bow to Japanese demands to prevent the massacre of so many innocent people.

Just hours after the tragedy at Pearl Harbor, the Japanese attacked American bases on Guam and Wake Island in the Pacific. The next day, December 8, they bombed Clark Field near Manila in the Philippines. In one swift raid, they destroyed half the planes of the U.S. Army's Far East Air Corps.

Two days later, Japanese soldiers began a land invasion of the Philippine Islands proper. The American and Filipino forces under General Douglas MacArthur fought valiantly, but they were no match for the huge number of Japanese soldiers. After putting up stiff resistance, they withdrew to the Bataan Peninsula on central Luzon in the Philippines. Here they held out with determination but were forced to surrender in April 1942. Some 10,000 escaped to the small, nearby island of Corregidor, where they fought on for another month. Before Bataan fell, President Roosevelt ordered that General MacArthur be secretly evacuated from the Philippines to Austra-lia by way of submarine. The president did not want one of America's leading generals to fall into the hands of the Japanese. MacArthur left, turning over his command to General Jonathan Wainwright. It was General Wainwright who surrendered Corregidor and all of the Philippines to the Japanese on May 6, 1942.

Nothing slowed down the massive advance of the Japanese. Between December 1941 and May 1942, they took Hong Kong and Singapore from the British. They invaded and took the East Indies (now Indonesia) from the Dutch. Having already wrested Indochina from French control in 1940, the Japanese broadened their hold on Southeast Asia by seizing Burma. Their conquest of Southeast Asia and the Malay Peninsula provided the Japanese with much-needed oil, rubber, and metals, as well as rice. At its height, the Japanese Empire extended from Burma to the Marshall Islands in the north Pacific.

Continued on page 11.

The Japanese Steamroller

Using an atlas, world map, or a map from your textbook, label the following places on the map of the Pacific Theater shown below.

Japan	Manchuria	Australia	Hong Kong	China	Hawaii
Singapore	Indochina	Guam	Burma	Wake Island	Netherlands or Dutch East Indies
Philippines				
Malay Peninsula				

Use with page 10.

ALEUTIAN ISLANDS

ALEUTIAN ISLANDS

• MIDWAY

PACIFIC OCEAN

IWO JIMA

MARIANAS

MARSHALL ISLANDS

KWAJALEIN

GILBERT ISLANDS

TARAWA

SOLOMAN ISLANDS

Coral Sea

Sea of Japan

Manila

BATAAN

South China Sea

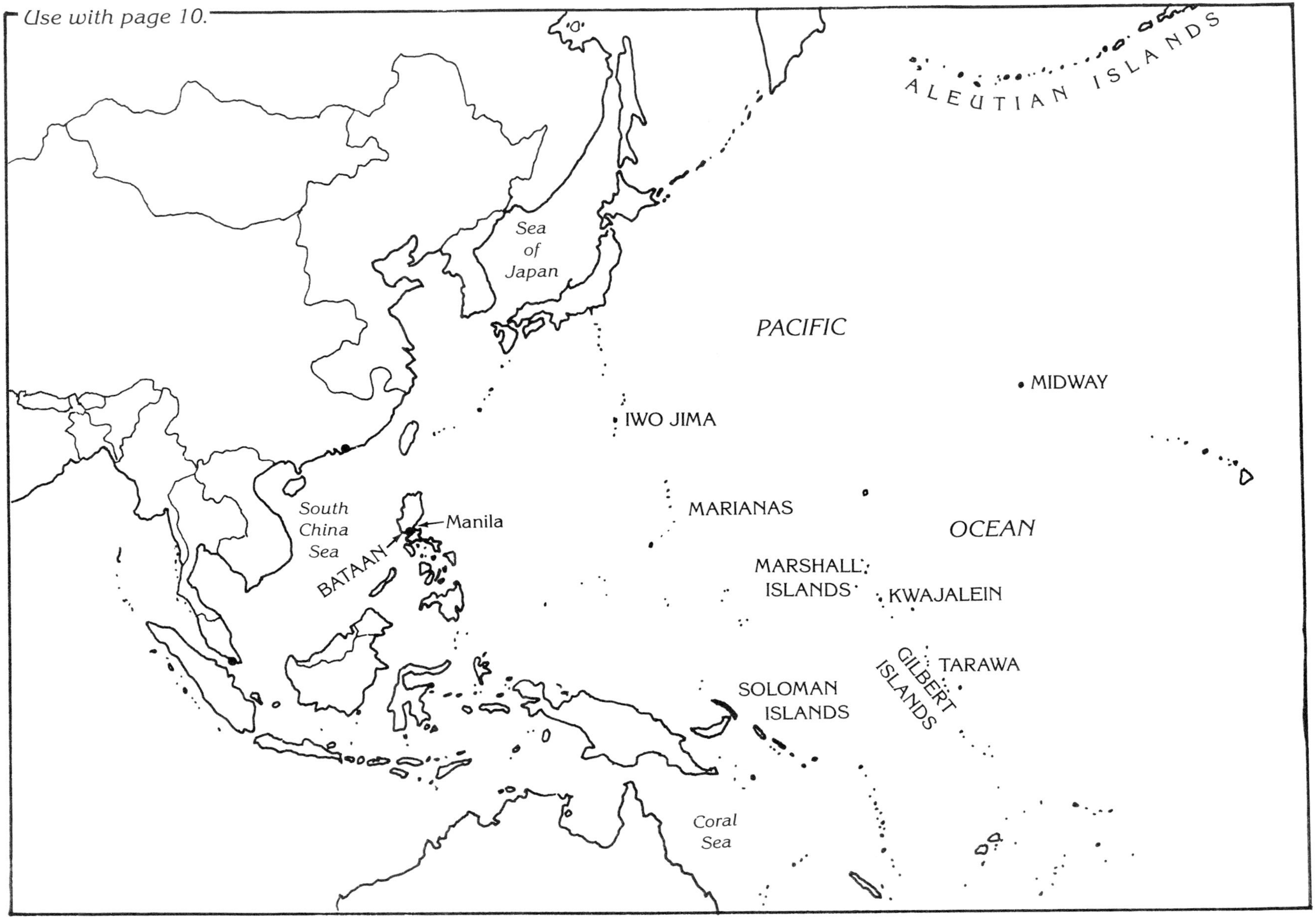

April 14, 1942

Dear Diary

Two months have passed since we arrived at the relocation center. We are herded together in wooden barracks covered with tar paper. The barracks are divided into family "apartments" measuring 20 by 25 feet, each heated by a pot-bellied stove. Last month was particularly cold, and Papa and some of the other men piled dirt against the side of our building to keep out the wind. Will spring ever come?

Despite the hardships, people go about their daily tasks believing that the government will soon realize its error in interning us and allow us to return to our homes. We young people are generally in high spirits, but our parents and other adults are bitter. Especially Papa. Papa worked hard all his life building a successful grocery business, and overnight, it was virtually stolen from him. Some men from the government came to the store in February and told Papa he had one week to get his affairs in order before all of us would be shipped to a special camp. Not wanting to lose everything, Papa quickly sold the store to an unscrupulous businessman for a third of its value.

Papa, however, says we were lucky compared to other Japanese-Americans. Some had only 48 hours to dispose of their homes and property. Lifestyles that took years to build were destroyed in a matter of days. And what's really ironic is that we Japanese-Americans, who, in the eyes of our government, can't be trusted, must still provide soldiers to fight in the United States Army! Just last week, two of our young men were drafted right out of camp! It is truly a strange world.

In the weeks following Pearl Harbor, a wave of hysteria swept across America. Rapid Japanese successes in the Pacific convinced many Americans that an enemy attack on the west coast was imminent. Such fear mushroomed into a hatred of everything Japanese and held dire consequences for thousands of innocent people.

In December 1941, approximately 127,000 residents of Japanese descent lived in the Pacific coast states of California, Oregon, and Washington. Of this number, two-thirds were citizens of the United States. These citizens considered themselves as loyal as other Americans. But the United States government thought otherwise. Fear of sabotage and cooperation with the enemy caused President Franklin Roosevelt to authorize the relocation of all Japanese living along the west coast to internment camps in remote areas of California, Utah, Wyoming, and other states. Almost overnight, an entire culture was uprooted and its people sent packing simply because of racial origin.

Most of the Japanese-Americans and Japanese aliens who were sent to the camps remained interned until the final months of the war. When they were finally released, they soon discovered they had little to go home to. Many had lost their homes, their businesses, their farms, and their jobs. Years later, with the help of a regretful U.S. government, they managed to recover about 10 per cent of their losses.

Discuss . . .

- how the United States could have better handled its fears of sabotage during World War II.

- why 8,000 young Japanese-American men—considering the treatment accorded their parents and others—would fight with distinction in the U.S. Army during the war, many receiving commendations for heroism and valor.

- how loyal Japanese citizens must have felt upon being sent to relocation centers.

- other incidents in American history during which fear and prejudice resulted in the mistreatment of a particular group of people.

The March of Death

Interview
October 1, 1945

Ques. "Colonel, were all Japanese officers and soldiers cruel and abusive toward prisoners of war?"

Ans. "Most were, but a few were kind and tried to help us. Some shared food, water, and cigarettes. I even know of incidents where Japanese guards released prisoners whom they were ordered to take out and shoot. They did this at great risk to their own lives."

Ques. "How, then, Colonel, can you account for the brutality of the majority of the guards?"

Ans. "I think it has to do with bushido, the Japanese warrior's code of conduct. The code considers it a disgrace to surrender. That is why most Japanese soldiers fought to the death. And because Americans surrender when all odds are against them, I believe the Japanese saw us as weak and not worthy of being spared. Whatever the reason, nothing can excuse the horrible atrocities they committed. I am happy to hear that those responsible will be brought to trial for their crimes."

The fate of the Americans and Filipinos who surrendered at Bataan was not fully known for three years. When the full story was finally revealed, the world was shocked and outraged.

On April 10, 1942, one day after Bataan fell, some 75,000 prisoners were assembled for a march to a prison camp 65 miles to the north. Even before the march began, some prisoners were shot or beheaded. Others were beaten senseless. Along the route to the camp, any prisoner who fell out of line and could not continue was shot or bayoneted. Some were even buried alive. Food was almost nonexistent and the only water allowed came from filthy ditches along the way. By the time the column reached Camp O'Donnell, at least 22,000 men had died or had been brutally killed. Thousands more died while in captivity.

Over 12,000 soldiers who surrendered at Corregidor on May 6 were also interned by the Japanese. First by freighter and then by train, they were transported to a camp at Cabanatuan, approximately 75 miles north of Manila. Over 2,000 died from hunger and disease during their first two months of confinement.

Discuss . . .

- whether all persons, regardless of rank, who participate in war atrocities should be held accountable for their crimes. Or should only those in command who issue the orders be punished?

- why soldiers in wartime might commit acts of violence they would otherwise not commit in times of peace.

- whether atrocities occur in every war, or if World War II was a singularly brutal conflict.

For Further Study

- Compare the treatment of American prisoners of war under the Japanese to that under the Germans.

- In what ways did the Japanese violate the rules set forth in the Geneva Convention regarding the treatment of prisoners of war?

Aboard the Hornet
April 1942

Dear Mom,

My hand is shaking as I write. At long last we know our mission. We are going to bomb Japan! Can you believe it? This is our response to the Japanese for what they did at Pearl Harbor and in the Philippines.

During those months of training at Eglin Air Force Base in Florida, we wondered about all the hours of practice spent taking off at slower speeds and over shorter distances. It never occurred to us that we were practicing to lift a bomber off the deck of an aircraft carrier! From the start, we knew we had volunteered to be part of an "unknown" mission, the details of which we would learn later. When they told us what we were going to do, you could have knocked me over with a feather! Imagine—taking off in a B-25 bomber in the middle of the ocean. That's a first I wouldn't have missed for anything.

Mom, I have to go. We have a briefing in a few minutes, and I'd best not be late. Take care, and don't worry about me.

Love,
Tex

P.S. For security purposes, this letter will be sent after the raid.

Nine days after the surrender of U.S. and Philippine troops on the Bataan Peninsula, American spirits were lifted by a startling announcement. On April 18, planes launched from an aircraft carrier 600 miles off the coast of Japan had bombed Tokyo and several other Japanese cities. The news was incredible.

A bombing raid of Japan utilizing regular carrier planes was not feasible early in the war. Not only did carrier planes have a limited range, but if an American aircraft carrier had ventured too close to the Japanese mainland early in 1942, it would have been blasted out of the water. An attack using medium-range bombers, however, had some possibility of succeeding.

The raid was carried out by sixteen B-25 bombers under the command of Lieutenant Colonel James Doolittle. The plan called for the planes to take off from the USS Hornet when the ship was 400 miles off the coast of Japan. But fear that the carrier had been spotted by Japanese surface vessels caused a change of plans: the bombers were to be launched one day early, in bad weather, and 200 miles farther out. Consequently, none of the planes had enough fuel to reach the airbases in China where they were scheduled to land following their missions. Except for one plane that landed in Soviet territory, all the rest crash-landed either in the sea or along the Chinese coast. A few crew members fell into Japanese hands, but most, including Colonel Doolittle, were rescued.

The positive effect of the raid on American morale was much more important than the limited damage inflicted by the bombs. For the first time in the war, Americans had something to cheer about.

Discuss . . .

- why Lieutenant Colonel Doolittle's raid was important, even though the risks were high and the chances of success low.

- what effect the raid may have had on the Japanese feeling of invincibility.

Journal Entry
Aboard the Nagara
June 8, 1942

We are sailing home to Japan, thoroughly beaten. If this journal is found in my possession, I am sure I will be courtmartialed and then executed. But my life is of no concern; I must tell this story, if only to myself.

I was with Admiral Nagumo aboard the Akagi before it was sunk by American torpedo bombers. On the first day of the battle, we were spotted by a torpedo squadron of 15 planes from one of the American aircraft carriers. For some reason, they had become separated from their escorts. Having no cover, one would think the Americans would have turned and run. They did not. Knowing they were probably going to die, the pilots of those planes attacked and dropped their torpedoes before our Zeros shot them from the sky. It seems likely that every one of those pilots died. So much for our propaganda that raves about the cowardliness of our enemy.

I don't know the severity of our losses, but I have heard that all four of our carriers were sunk. If that is true, it is a devastating blow to Japan.

Japan's swift and unchallenged march through Asia and the Pacific came to an end in the spring of 1942. For the first time in the war, the Japanese were defeated and turned back.

On May 4, 1942, a large Japanese convoy was detected steaming toward Port Moresby in New Guinea. A successful assault on New Guinea would open the way for an invasion of Australia. And if Australia fell to the Japanese, the demoralizing effect on the Allies would be considerable.

Planes from the American carriers *Yorktown* and *Lexington* ensured that an invasion of Australia never materialized. On May 4, pilots sank several Japanese troop ships. Then, three days later, they took part in the only battle in naval history fought entirely by planes from aircraft carriers. No ship on either side fired a single shot at an enemy vessel. In what was called the *Battle of the Coral Sea*, American planes sank the Japanese light carrier *Shoho* and severely damaged two large carriers, the *Shokaku* and the *Zuikaku*. The United States lost the carrier *Lexington*. The battle was far from a decisive American victory, but it saved Australia from invasion. The Japanese fleet turned and sailed home to Japan to nurse its wounds.

One month later, the Japanese fleet was on the move again, determined to destroy American sea power in the Pacific. They also wanted to exact revenge on the United States for the Doolittle raid that had taken place in April. Their destination was Midway Island at the tip of the Hawaiian chain. To divert attention from their real goal, the Japanese attacked Attu in the Aleutian Islands at

Continued on page 16.

Continued from page 15.

the same time. Their ultimate aim was to take Midway and use it as a springboard to invade Hawaii.

The Japanese had no way of knowing their plans were doomed to failure. Three weeks before the Midway operation, American cryptologists had broken the Japanese code. Not only did the United States know about the impending strike at Midway, but they were aware of the diversionary attack in the Aleutians as well. As soon as the message revealing Japanese intentions was intercepted, the U.S. Pacific fleet swung into action.

Planes from four American carriers flew out to locate the Japanese armada. Several squadrons searched without success and returned to their carriers or air fields on Midway. Finally, Torpedo Squadron 8 from the *Hornet* located the enemy fleet on the morning of June 4 and reported its position by radio. Then the 15 planes of the squadron attacked the carriers in what amounted to a suicide mission. All were shot down, and only one pilot was rescued.

The ensuing battle of Midway raged for two days. When it was over, the Japanese had suffered a disastrous defeat. Four of their carriers—*Akagi, Kaga, Soryu,* and *Hiryu*—were sunk. The Japanese also lost several other ships and over 330 planes. About 2,500 Japanese sailors and pilots were killed. American losses were severe but not as heavy. One U.S. destroyer and the carrier *Yorktown* were sunk, while about 150 planes were shot down. Over 300 Americans lost their lives.

The Battle of Midway was the turning point of the war against the Japanese in the Pacific. In its wake, Allied forces went on the offensive. It was to be a slow and laborious process. It took the Allied forces more than two years to recover the territories which the Japanese had overrun in only six months.

Discuss . . .

- why battleships did not play a central role in the battles of the Coral Sea and Midway.
- whether naval engagements of the future will involve planes from carriers or simply be fought with missiles.
- how the war in the Pacific might have turned out had the United States not broken the Japanese code before Midway.

Guadalcanal

Guadalcanal
September 10, 1942

Dear Uncle Bill,

This is the first chance I've had to write since I came ashore last month. Needless to say, I've been quite busy.

Before I left the States, you asked me to let you know what it is like fighting the Japanese—if they are anything like the Germans you fought in France in 1918. Well, I think it's safe to say there is no comparison. Japanese soldiers just will not surrender. If they see things aren't going their way, they will stab themselves or make a crazy suicide charge. Why? I'm told they consider it a disgrace to surrender. I guess that is why they hold on to every pillbox and cave until the very end.

Don't mention any of this to Mom and Dad. So far, I've told them that the worst things we have to face here are leeches and scorpions. I don't want them to sit around and worry about me. Take care of yourself, and drop me a line when you can.

Your "favorite" nephew,
Don

Guadalcanal was the first in a series of "island hopping" campaigns in which the Allies slowly worked their way northward through the Pacific toward the Japanese mainland. The battle for Guadalcanal overlapped a fierce struggle in New Guinea, where a combined force of Americans and Australians inflicted the first land defeat of the war on the Japanese. In New Guinea, the Japanese landed 15,000 troops near the New Guinean capital of Port Moresby in July. Their goal, as during the Battle of the Coral Sea, was to use New Guinea as a base to invade Australia. Once again, they failed.

U.S. Marines invaded Guadalcanal in the Solomon Islands on August 7, 1942. Heavy fighting raged for six months, not only on land but in the air and at sea as well. By the time the fighting was over, the United States had lost two cruisers and seven destroyers, and almost 1,600 troops. The Japanese suffered 15,000 dead in the jungles and mountains of the island alone. Thousands more were lost at sea and in the air. Their defeat ended the threat to Australia and put the Japanese on the defensive for the remainder of the war.

After Guadalcanal, the Allies seized control of the other islands in the Solomon chain. By November 1943, the Americans had reached Bougainville, where the long and arduous trek to the north would finally end with the defeat of the Japanese in March of 1944.

Discuss . . .

- why it would take three long years for the Allies to advance through the Pacific islands held by the Japanese.
- how you feel about the Japanese soldier's preference to take his own life rather than surrender.
- likely reasons why the Allies did not simply bypass all the Pacific islands held by the Japanese and invade Japan directly.

Journal Entry
Aboard the Puffer
October 10, 1943

We have been at a depth of 500 feet under the sea for over 20 hours. I worry that I might go completely mad. That is why I have opened my journal and started to write. Although I find it hard to concentrate, I feel that writing is my only hope of maintaining sanity.

Our ordeal started before dawn when we torpedoed a Japanese merchant ship. As we maneuvered into position to fire several more shots at it, a Japanese submarine chaser located us and began dropping its depth charges. Hour after hour it circled above, hurling more depth charges and forcing us to dive deeper and deeper. After some time, a second submarine chaser joined the first and the number of depth charges doubled. Some charges exploded so close that the Puffer began to take on water. Eventually we descended to our present depth, which is 200 feet deeper than this submarine should go. That is where we are now and where we hope to ride this thing out.

The air inside is now stale and stifling. With the air conditioning and blowers shut off to reduce giveaway noises, we can hardly breathe. Everyone is sweating profusely, and some of the men have become dehydrated. Any water they drink to ease their suffering is vomited back up again.

The oppressive heat and unbearable conditions are taking their toll in other ways. Men are beginning to lash out at one another. They talk of their hatred for the navy, the submarine service, and the Japanese. Nerves are on edge and tempers are short. We jump at every little sound we hear, and the terror shows in our faces each time a depth charge explodes above us. I'm sure we'd be at each other's throats if we only had the energy to do it.

As I check the time, it is now 1400 hours (2 A.M.). We have been down almost 21 hours. How much longer can we endure? How much longer can this sub stand these depths before it collapses? Are we destined for a watery grave, never to see our loved ones again—never to be found?

While thousands of Americans were fighting the Japanese on land, in the air, and on the sea, a comparatively smaller number were fighting the enemy under the sea. These were the men of the submarine service. Their contributions to victory were immense. United States submarines were responsible for sinking 55 per cent of all ships lost by the Japanese during the war. Even the *Puffer*, written about in the journal entry above, survived its ordeal and went on to sink 8 enemy ships. The number of Japanese vessels sunk by American submarines exceeded the combined totals registered by surface ships, carrier planes, and army air corps bombers.

Continued on page 19.

The War Under the Sea

Continued from page 18.

When the war against Japan began, the United States had only 55 submarines in its Pacific fleet. Nearly half of these were either obsolete, in dry dock for repairs, or assigned to other duties. The situation was grim. Other than the three carriers that were not at Pearl Harbor when the Japanese attacked on December 7, 1941, this woefully small number of submarines was about all America had left with which to fight the enemy.

But fight the enemy they did! No one, not even the Japanese, could have predicted the ferocity with which American submariners would fight. As the number of boats at their disposal increased, so too did the number of enemy vessels they sank. By war's end, American submarines had sunk more than 1,300 Japanese ships. Over 1,100 of these were large merchant vessels laden with supplies and raw materials Japan greatly needed.

This war's U.S. submarine warfare did not begin so successfully, however. In 1942, the first year United States submarines were active in the Pacific, they sank only two major enemy combat ships. The Japanese, on the other hand, scored heavily in the early months of the war. The American carriers they sank were the *Yorktown*, *Wasp*, and *Saratoga*. The Japanese also sank or damaged scores of other American ships.

The year 1943 saw a change in American tactics. Submarines began to hunt in wolf packs consisting of three or four boats, and the results became quickly apparent. More than 300 Japanese ships were sent to the bottom of the ocean. By the end of 1944, so many enemy ships had been destroyed that American submarines were hard-pressed to find any more to attack. Still, there were sinkings that went on right up to the day the Japanese surrendered—August 14, 1945.

The destruction wrought by United States submarines in the Pacific crushed Japan's economy and hastened the end of the war. But the price paid by America for this achievement was staggering—52 submarines were sunk and 3,505 submariners were killed.

Discuss . . .

- why you would or would not volunteer to serve on a submarine.
- what personal characteristics would best serve someone assigned to submarine duty.
- whether the contributions of the submarine service were equal to or superior to those of the other armed services.

For Further Study

Research the *Turtle*, America's first submarine. It was used in the Revolutionary War. Compare it with the submarines of World War II.

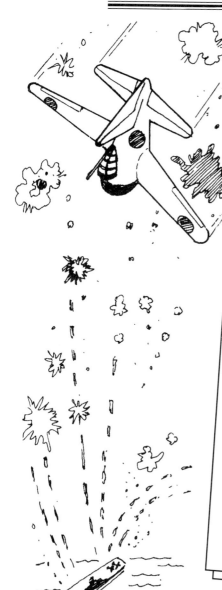

July 10, 1944
Saipan

Dear Diary,

I thought I had seen everything until recently when several thousand drunken Japanese came at us in a wild suicide charge. Some had guns; others wielded swords and knives; a few were armed with broken bottles and baseball bats. Some had no weapon at all. It was kill or be killed. Not a single Japanese soldier survived that madness. We lost quite a few men ourselves.

But that suicide attack was nothing compared to what happened at the cliffs today. Apparently believing Japanese government propaganda that all civilians would be executed by us Americans, I saw Japanese mothers hurl their children from the cliffs to the rocks below, and then jump off themselves. I watched in disbelief as other civilians cut their own throats or blew themselves up with hand grenades, bowing discreetly to us before doing so. I saw entire families hold hands and walk to a drowning death into the sea. And I will never forget one young boy who sat for a long time on the rocks trying to muster enough courage to throw himself into the water. When he finally did, he flailed about frantically, proving that the desire to live is inherent even in those thinking they wish to die.

Throughout this macabre scene, there was nothing we could do but stand there, staring in horror.

The epidemic of wartime Japanese suicides reached horrifying heights when U.S. troops invaded the island of Saipan. The actions of the Japanese illustrate the tenacity with which the Japanese fought and points to their pervading belief that American troops would assault or kill any person who fell into their hands.

Many battles, however, had to be fought by the U.S. before Saipan could be reached. From the Solomons, the U.S. Marines moved on to the Gilbert Islands in the central Pacific. The best known of the Gilberts is Tarawa, the site of one of the bloodiest battles of the Pacific war.

Tarawa, in reality, is an atoll composed of a number of small islands. Betio Island, because it contained an airstrip, was the most heavily defended by the enemy. Here, in November 1943, more than 4,500 well-entrenched Japanese awaited the arrival of some 12,000 American Marines. In four days of heavy fighting, the Marines took the island, but the price of wiping out heavily fortified pillboxes was high. The United States suffered about 1,000 dead and about 2,200 wounded. As for the Japanese, most of those who were not killed committed suicide. Only 17 of the 4,500 defenders of Betio Island were taken prisoner.

Continued on page 21.

Continued from page 20.

After securing the Gilberts, U.S. troops assaulted the Marshall Islands, located near the equator. In February 1944, they landed on Kwajalein and took it in seven days. Ten days later, they came ashore on Enewetak, capturing it in four days. Allied military leaders decided to forego the capture of Truk in the Carolines, a strategic Japanese naval base. Instead, they bombed it, rendering it useless as a base. The way was now clear to the Mariana Islands, located about 2,000 miles from Japan.

The Marianas was the scene of some of the Pacific's bloodiest fighting. Many Marines gave their lives in assaults on Tinian, Saipan, and Guam. Especially severe were the struggles to take the latter two. U.S. Marines landed on Saipan on June 15, 1944, and did not take the island until July 9. Over 16,000 Americans were killed or wounded. The capture of Saipan was important because it put the United States within striking distance of Japan.

Guam, the largest of the Mariana Islands, was invaded on July 21 but was not captured until August 10, after bitter fighting. American casualties were heavy at first because, after landing on the beaches, they were subjected to intense

Japanese artillery fire from cliffs high above. Once these weapons were disabled, the island was taken rather quickly. The climax of the fighting came with a Japanese suicide charge similar to the one at Saipan. Although the island was declared taken on July 9, some Japanese held out in the hills for weeks, and a few even for years.

From the Marianas, the American forces moved next to Peleliu in the Palau Islands, only 600 miles east of the Philippines. They landed on September 15 and met resistance much stiffer than expected. The 10,000 Japanese troops on the island had dug into a series of coral caves and pillboxes and had to be pried out. Before the battle ended, Peleliu cost the lives of another 1,500 Americans. But most of the "island hopping" campaigns had gratefully come to an end. Only two remained to be fought—Iwo Jima and Okinawa.

Discuss . . .

- the psychological effects of fighting a fanatical foe like the Japanese in World War II.
- how propaganda can completely alter the beliefs and behavior of a people.

For Further Study

Locate the Solomon, Gilbert, Caroline, Marshall, and Mariana Islands on a map of the Pacific. Calculate the approximate distance of each from Japan.

July 12, 1944

The Seabees

TINIAN—I have seen and experienced everything now.

Due to my clumsiness, I fell and broke my dentures shortly after arriving on Tinian. Immediately, I panicked. Was I destined to "gum" my way across the Pacific, subsisting on rice and oatmeal as I wandered from island to island?

The next day, as I sat in my tent pondering my fate, a jaunty Seabee appeared and delivered me from my culinary dilemma.

"Say fella," he began, "I hear you broke your choppers."

"Yeah," I lamented, "and I'm just about to starve to death."

"No problem," my savior assured me. "I can have you chewing on a thick steak in no time."

"Chewing on a steak in no time? How?" I questioned. The newly arrived creative Seabee quickly showed me. I watched with some doubt as he concocted a strange mixture of

ground rubber and cement and glued my shattered dental plates back together.

"Now," he concluded, "I'll leave this little baby in a vise overnight, and tomorrow you'll be able to bite a bullet in two."

Sure enough, the next day, my false teeth were as good as new, and I was once more a force to be reckoned with in the mess tent.

Amazing fellows, these Seabees.

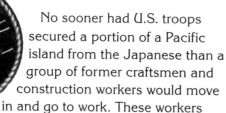

No sooner had U.S. troops secured a portion of a Pacific island from the Japanese than a group of former craftsmen and construction workers would move in and go to work. These workers were units of the Seabees, or the U.S. Navy's Construction Battalions. They were called Seabees because the initials for Construction Battalion are *C.B.*

The Seabees were commissioned in March 1942, and were attached to the U.S. Navy. The Seabees included machinists, engineers, electricians, plumbers, and carpenters. Their work was dangerous, and, although they had received no formal military training, they often fought Japanese troops in the performance of their duties.

One of the most important Seabee projects was to construct airstrips from which American bombers would take off enroute to Japan. The task was often monumental. First, trees and stumps had to be

removed with bulldozers. Then, the cleared earth was leveled and covered with interlocking strips of steel. Finally, crushed coral was spread on top of the steel and wet down to form a hard surface. And all the while, the Seabees might have been under fire from nearby Japanese troops. Impossible as it may sound, the Seabees could construct one of these airstrips in as short a time as three weeks.

Besides airstrips, the Seabees constructed roads, bridges, barracks, hospitals, fuel tanks, and floating pontoon docks. There was hardly a project the Seabees would not tackle. They even repaired wristwatches by replacing broken crystals with plexiglass from downed airplanes. One ingenious Seabee went so far as to create a pair of insignia stars out of U.S. quarters for a general.

The motto of the Seabees was "Can do!" For three years in the Pacific, it was a motto they proudly lived up to. Their contribution to the war effort in the Pacific cannot be overstated.

Discuss . . .

- why 260,000 Americans would join an organization such as the Seabees. Think of as many reasons as you can.

- which group had the more difficult task in your opinion: the engineers who built the Burma Road or the Seabees who served in the Pacific. Explain why.

In the Philippines
October 25, 1944

My dear parents,

    I have completed my letters. I have given my belongings to friends. Tomorrow I drink a ceremonial cup of saki with my commander and then take off on my mission. Tomorrow I die for my Emperor and my country.

    I am, at the moment, very happy. In fact, these last few weeks have been among the happiest of my life. I have read, enjoyed the company of my friends, and composed poems to my Emperor. Everyone here has been wonderful. Yesterday, upon inspecting my plane, I noticed that the cockpit had been polished to a high shine. Upon inquiring of one of the ground crew why he had gone to such pains, he stated that he wanted my plane to serve as a coffin worthy of one about to give his life for his country. When I thanked him for his effort, he was moved to tears. So was I.

    Do not grieve for me, my parents. I am honored to play such an important role in the defense of our empire. I thank my superiors for giving me the opportunity to die in such a glorious manner. What more can a samurai ask for?

    I will die with your names on my lips. Say goodbye to my brothers and sisters for me.

Your son,
Takijiro

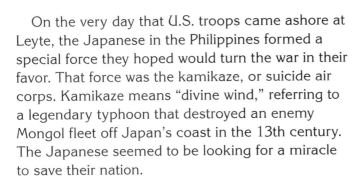

On the very day that U.S. troops came ashore at Leyte, the Japanese in the Philippines formed a special force they hoped would turn the war in their favor. That force was the kamikaze, or suicide air corps. Kamikaze means "divine wind," referring to a legendary typhoon that destroyed an enemy Mongol fleet off Japan's coast in the 13th century. The Japanese seemed to be looking for a miracle to save their nation.

There was no shortage of volunteers to fly the kamikaze planes. Young Japanese pilots jumped at the opportunity to steer an explosive-laden Zero into the side or deck of an American ship. Many volunteered for religious or patriotic reasons, while others, convinced they were destined to die anyway, wanted to go out in a blaze of glory.

The kamikazes first saw action in the Battle of Leyte Gulf on October 25, 1944. During the ensuing struggle for the Philippines, they destroyed 16 ships and damaged no fewer than 80 others. This could not compare, however, to the havoc they would wreak at the Battle of Okinawa several months later. At Okinawa, 1,000 kamikazes sank over 30 American vessels. But despite their heroics and the destruction they caused, the kamikazes did not change the outcome of the war.

Discuss . . .

- what kinds of personal traits kamikaze pilots had to possess.
- how the families of kamikaze pilots could accept their deaths in a stoic manner.
- why the kamikaze attacks were so alien to, and in conflict with, Western philosophy.
- what psychological effect a successful kamikaze attack might have on an enemy crew.

Journal Entry
Santo Tomás University, Manila
February 6, 1945

At last we are free! Soldiers from the American First Cavalry Division liberated the camp three days ago. Words could not describe our joy and happiness as we watched those Yanks chase the Japanese off our island. I planted a great, big kiss on the first Yankee soldier I encountered!

Even though, of course, I feel happy, I also feel a bit nervous and unsettled. It seems so strange that I now enjoy the freedom to do things I couldn't do for so long, such as write in my diary. I was afraid of what might happen to my family if the Japanese caught me writing about the war.

My parents and I—along with 3,700 other British and American civilians—have been interned at Santo Tomás for three years. But it seems as though my entire life has been spent in captivity. In 1942, I was a carefree 12-year-old. Now, at 15, I sometimes feel older than my years—as if my youth has slipped away. I'm sure this feeling will pass once I am accustomed to freedom again.

In spite of my mixed emotions, overall I realize that I am a very lucky person. Several of my friends died at Santo Tomás of malnutrition. I might have been among them were it not for the generosity and self-sacrifice of my parents. They shared their small food rations with me. I felt guilty each time I took food from their bowls, but I was always so hungry! Mother and Father must have been hungry all the time. Father, who is a large man, must have lost 75 pounds in the camp. He now looks skeletal. Mother, who has always been rather thin, looks as though the wind could blow her away. I truly appreciate what they did for me. How much they must love me!

The liberation of the Philippines took months of hard fighting. U.S. soldiers met stiff resistance on every island, as the Japanese, even with no hope of victory, often fought fanatically to the last man. Although Manila was taken in February 1945, enemy resistance continued well into the summer. The loss of the Philippines cut the Japanese empire in two and cost the emperor 400,000 of his best troops. At least 14,000 American soldiers died retaking the island, while 48,000 came up wounded or missing.

As American soldiers fought their way through the Philippines, they liberated a number of prison camps. Santo Tomás University in Manila, mentioned in the diary entry above, was one. Although the inmates of the camp were not harmed as the Americans approached, the Filipino civilians in the city itself were not so fortunate. Of the 700,000 residents of Manila, close to 100,000 Filipinos died during the Japanese defense and retreat from Manila.

Discuss . . .

- what life might be like for young people inside a prison camp.

- what personal characteristics might better enable an individual to withstand the brutal treatment and hardships of a prison camp.

- whether you, as a prison internee, would share your rationed provisions with another person. Why or why not?

February 4, 1945
Kunming, China

Dear Folks,

They said it couldn't be done. But, by George, we did it! We brought in the first supplies to China over the Ledo-Burma Road.

I was in one of the first trucks to pass through Kunming's city gates. People were everywhere, cheering and waving flags. There was a huge banner that read "The Road to Victory." I felt proud. I had helped to accomplish a feat so many people said was impossible. Even old Winston Churchill in England had his doubts. Well, maybe he'll swallow his cigar when he hears of our success!

Have to go. There is a small ceremony planned to recognize the success of the road.

Love,
Henry

The retaking of the Philippines made it possible for the United States to step up its bombing of Japanese cities. Raids became more frequent, and the Japanese, with most of their air and naval power destroyed, could do little to stop the Americans. The Japanese capital of Tokyo was the primary target.

In the meantime, heavy fighting was taking place in China and Burma. The Allies knew they could bypass China and assault Japan directly from the Philippines, but it was vital to keep China in the war. A well-supplied Chinese army would keep thousands of Japanese troops pinned down—troops that could otherwise be used elsewhere.

To keep China in the war, it was necessary to re-open and add to the Burma Road. When the Japanese seized Burma in 1942 and cut this route, the only way left to supply China was by dangerous flights across the Himalaya Mountains. So American engineers began the Ledo-Burma

Road project. The Ledo-Burma Road began in Ledo in the Indian state of Assam and hooked up with the old Burma Road. The combined supply line covered more than 1,100 mountainous miles from Ledo to Kunming, China. Engineers and work crews completed it in January 1945, after two years during which they battled disease, rains, and Japanese troops. After a short time, the Ledo-Burma Road was renamed the Stilwell Road after General Joseph Stilwell, commander of Allied forces in the China-Burma-India theater. Over 5,000 trucks carried 34,000 tons of supplies to China during the seven months the road was in operation.

Combined forces of American, British, Chinese, and Indian troops fought the Japanese in Burma. On May 3, 1945, British Commonwealth troops took Rangoon, the capital, and Burma once again was in Allied hands. The Japanese were on the run everywhere.

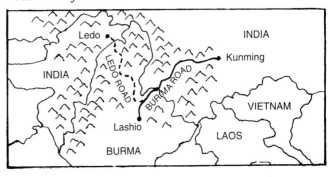

For Further Study

Look at a map of Asia and locate the following:

   (1) the Himalaya Mountains

   (2) India in relation to Burma

   (3) the direction in which the Ledo-Burma Road runs from Lashio, Burma, to Kunming, China

Iwo Jima
February 20, 1945

I am one of the lucky ones. Many of my buddies didn't make it. They are still lying on the beach or in the surf where they fell.

It didn't seem so bad when we first came ashore yesterday morning. There was only sporadic fire from the Japanese, and we thought everything would be okay. We had no way of knowing, of course, that the Japanese were purposely letting several thousand of us onto the beach before they really opened fire. When they did, it was a living nightmare. The big guns on Mount Suribachi and the machine guns and mortars hidden in the caves and pillboxes raked the beach from one side to the other. Guys fell like limp dolls in the black sand. As long as I live, I will never forget the agonized screams of the wounded and dying.

Since there was little cover on the beach, we had no choice but to crawl forward in the face of that murderous fire. Gradually, by nightfall, we made it to an airfield, and things settled down a bit. I understand that some units lost 70 per cent of their men yesterday morning. We know now that taking Iwo Jima won't be easy.

One of the last battles of the Pacific war was fought at Iwo Jima. It was also one of the most costly in terms of casualties.

Iwo Jima is a small island between Guam and Japan. Its location, only 750 miles from Japan, made it desirable as an Allied air base. Knowing this, the Japanese built an almost impregnable fortress on the island. Twenty-one thousand Japanese troops dug into a system of tunnels, pillboxes, and caves and waited for the Americans to arrive.

When the Marines landed on February 19, 1945, they met resistance as stiff as any they had faced in the war. Seventy-five days of previous bombardment had had little effect on the enemy. Although Mount Suribachi was taken on February 23 and the American flag was raised at its summit, fighting continued for twenty-six days afterwards. Estimates of American casualties ranged from 4,000 to 7,000 killed and from 15,000 to 19,000 wounded. Of the 21,000 Japanese defending Iwo Jima, only about 200 were taken prisoner. The others died by the thousands in caves and pillboxes that the Americans attacked with flamethrowers and hand grenades.

After Iwo Jima, one last island remained to be taken before an assault on the Japanese mainland was possible. That island was Okinawa.

Discuss . . .

- whether it was a wise decision to invade Iwo Jima when the United States had already secured bases on Saipan and in the Philippines from which to bomb Japan.
- what must have been the thoughts of an American Marine getting ready to hit the beach at Iwo Jima.
- how well such defensive structures as concrete pillboxes and blockouses would stand up to today's sophisticated weaponry.

Journal Entry
Aboard the USS Essex, Okinawa
April 8, 1945

Well, here we go again. Six months ago at Leyte Gulf, we were introduced to that demon of the sky—the Japanese kamikaze. But Leyte Gulf was a picnic compared to Okinawa. The Japanese have sent wave after wave of kamikazes against our ships. They know there are at least 50 American carriers that supported the invasion force, and they seem determined to sink every one of them. They are also going after other ships. A number of these have already been sunk and many more are damaged.

The Japanese know the importance of Okinawa. It is only 350 miles from their southernmost island, Kyushu. They know we need Okinawa to launch a land invasion of their country. That is why they are using every weapon they have against us.

Two days ago, the Japanese even sacrificed the Yamato, the largest battleship ever built. They apparently sent it to Okinawa hoping to lure more of our carriers close enough for kamikaze planes flying from Kyushu and Formosa to attack them. The Yamato had no air support at all, since the remainder of the Japanese carrier force had been destroyed at Leyte. I understand that planes from the USS Bennington sank the Yamato in a matter of minutes.

We are told that the marines and the army are involved in fierce fighting on the island. My heart and prayers go out to them.

Okinawa was the last great land battle fought during World War II. By the time it ended on June 22, 1945, Nazi Germany had surrendered, and the war in Europe was over.

The U.S. Navy and the U.S. Army Air Corps began aerial bombardments of Okinawa on March 18, 1945. Two weeks later, on April 1, a combined force of American Marines and soldiers landed and moved steadily inland. They met little or no resistance until the third day, when the Japanese launched their first real attack. More than eleven weeks of the bloodiest fighting in the Pacific followed. As on Iwo Jima, the Japanese were well-prepared and ready to fight to the last man.

Suicide attacks were frequent and resulted in many American casualties. More than 12,000 Americans gave their lives at Okinawa, many on ships that were hit by the kamikazes. General Simon Buckner, the commander of the combined invasion force, was killed. He was the highest-ranking American general killed in World War II.

Naval losses off Okinawa were staggering. The kamikazes sank 36 American ships and damaged almost 300 others. Nearly 5,000 American sailors died as the U.S. Navy suffered its worse punishment in history. But the island of Okinawa was secured, and America's military leaders began planning the long-awaited invasion of Japan itself.

Discuss . . .

- whether, considering the number of American casualties suffered at Okinawa, some less costly plan might have been devised to take the island. If so, what?

- the relationship that exists today between Japan and the United States.

Planned Invasion of Japan

Okinawa
July 4, 1945

Dear Curly,

Well, it's the 4th of July, but I won't be setting off any firecrackers in celebration. I've seen enough "fireworks" over the last few years to last a lifetime.

Things are finally quiet on Okinawa. I'm sure plans must be in the works now for an invasion of Japan. It's funny—I'm sitting here thumbing through my copy of a "Guide to the Western Pacific," a quaint little book that was issued to us last year. (It'll never make the Best Sellers' List!) There is a section on Kyushu, where an invasion could likely take place since the island is only 350 miles from Okinawa. The section warns us to watch out for earthquakes, bad drinking water, ticks, spiders, and a 20-inch poisonous snake called the mamushi. The last paragraph, almost an afterthought, warns us to also watch out for Japanese civilians. The book hints that they might pose a problem for us. What an understatement!

If I have to go ashore in southern Japan, the possibility of shooting civilians armed with bamboo spears is troublesome. But I suppose I would do it if it comes down to that. I just don't understand this fanaticism of the Japanese. Why don't they give up? As you know, they simply ignored Roosevelt's and then Truman's call for surrender. It looks like we're just going to have to go in and fight hard for every inch of Japanese soil.

Well, Curly, that's all for now. I hope to be home soon. After Guadalcanal and Okinawa, Japan should be a piece of cake.

Your brother,
Ben

The invasion of Japan was to consist of two separate attacks. The first, an assault on the southernmost island, Kyushu, was scheduled for November 1945. The second attack was to take place in March 1946, and would involve an invasion of Honshu, Japan's most populated island.

Military planners estimated the assault on Japan could cost as many as one million American and several million Japanese lives.

Besides the fanatical resistance of the Japanese military, civilians throughout Japan had been trained in the use of a variety of weapons, including such simple devices as sharpened bamboo spears. In addition, the Japanese had almost 1,600 kamikaze planes based on Kyushu to resist any American attack. A land invasion of Japan would be costly.

Discuss . . .

- whether an invasion of Japan would have resulted in as many fatalities as predicted.

For Further Study

Consult a map of Japan and answer the questions below.

(1) Which four islands make up the nation of Japan?

(2) What is the capital of Japan? Why do you think the bomb wasn't dropped on it?

(3) On which island is Hiroshima? Nagasaki? Which island is larger? Research further to find out why the atom bombs were dropped on these cities.

Journal Entry
Hiroshima Red Cross Hospital
August 13, 1945

It has been one week since most of Hiroshima was destroyed—by what, no one knows for certain. I have heard some doctors and nurses say that American bombers sprayed the city with gasoline and then somehow set it on fire. Some say it was a huge bomb. It matters little. With so many deaths and so much suffering, the actual cause of this catastrophe doesn't seem important.

I am one of the few to survive, although I suffer from burns over most of my body. My parents and sisters, I assume, are dead. I understand nothing remains of our home near the school or of my father's shop next to the railroad station. As I lay here thinking of my family I feel guilty for having survived.

The bomb—or whatever it was—fell on us at 8:15 in the morning. Professor Kozuka had just started his lecture on the solar system when the roof of our school collapsed and all the windows blew out. In seconds, the school was ablaze. Of the 210 students in the building, only 20 of us survived.

I ran into the street and made my way to the Sakae Bridge. People whose clothes were on fire and whose skin was horribly burned were throwing themselves into the river in an attempt to ease their agony. I too plunged into the water seeking relief for my burning skin.

Bodies littered the streets everywhere. Most were charred beyond recognition. Some were petrified in suspended motion. The living staggered along in a daze, their eyebrows burned off and burned flesh hanging from their faces and hands. These scenes will be etched into my memory forever.

Here at the Red Cross Hospital, medicine, bandages, and anesthetics are in short supply. Hundreds of people die painful deaths every day, and there is little the doctors and nurses can do to help.

Who knows what the future holds for me? At least I am alive.

Long before an invasion of Japan was planned, scientists in the United States were working on the most powerful weapon ever conceived. That weapon was the atomic bomb. In July 1945, the first atomic bomb was detonated in the desert near Alamogordo, New Mexico. Scientists who worked on it were not certain about what to expect when it exploded. Some thought it might blow up the state of New Mexico and beyond. A few even worried that the bomb might destroy the world.

President Franklin Roosevelt had died on April 12, 1945, and was succeeded by Vice-President Harry Truman. The new president knew of the atomic bomb and began weighing the consequences of its use. On the one hand, the bomb would kill thousands of innocent people in any city on which it was dropped. These people would die horrible, agonizing deaths. But on the other, not using the bomb and not going ahead with an invasion of Japan, could cause the war to drag on

Continued on page 30.

Continued from page 29.

for another year, possibly costing millions more Japanese and American lives.

President Truman listened to the advice of those who supported using the bomb. He also listened to opponents of the bomb, who believed that Japan was on the verge of surrendering and that the use of such a destructive weapon was not necessary. Having heard both sides, the president then made one of the most difficult decisions ever made by a head of state: he would, if necessary, use the atomic bomb against Japan. The president knew it was a decision that would draw the criticism of many. But he felt in his heart that the decision was the correct one.

Days before the first atomic bomb was dropped on Japan, American planes dropped leaflets warning the Japanese people of a terrible new weapon that would be used against them if their leaders did not end the fighting. But the Japanese militarists held steadfast and refused to surrender. When it was apparent that they had no intention of surrendering, the decision was made to use the bomb.

On August 6, 1945, a B-29 called the *Enola Gay* dropped the first atomic bomb ever used on humans. It destroyed one-half of the city of Hiroshima and killed more than 80,000 people. The bomb was so powerful that it completely leveled an area of 4.4 square miles at the center where it detonated.

Even with the terrible destruction at Hiroshima, the Japanese still refused to surrender. Three days later, another B-29 called *Bock's Car* dropped the second atomic bomb on the city of Nagasaki. It killed as many as 40,000 people. Finally, Japan's military leaders had had enough. They surrendered on August 14. After six long, terrible years, World War II was over.

Discuss . . .

- whether America's use of the atomic bomb against Japan was justified.
- whether you think Japan was ready to surrender in the summer of 1945.
- what decision you would have made concerning the use of the second atomic bomb had you been President Truman. Explain.
- whether you think future wars will involve the use of nuclear weapons.
- the feasibility of a terrorist group gaining access to a nuclear bomb today.

Surrender and Aftermath

Aboard the USS Missouri
September 2, 1945

Dear Connie,

It is over. Three years, eight months, and twenty-five days after Pearl Harbor, the Japanese have officially surrendered. I felt honored to witness the signing of the surrender documents. Standing on deck with the Missouri's other officers, I felt a lump in my throat as I watched history being made.

General MacArthur opened the ceremonies with a short speech. Then he stepped aside and the Japanese delegates signed the papers. They looked tense and a little out of place. As the Japanese signed, I watched General Wainwright as he stood behind General MacArthur. I understand that General Wainwright was invited as a special guest because of the treatment he suffered at the hands of the Japanese. What satisfaction he must have felt to see his captors of three years humbled at last.

I don't know when the Missouri will return to the States. Soon, I hope. I'm just thankful that the war's finally over and I made it through in one piece. As I write this, my thoughts are of you, and I will count the days until we are together again. Until then, hold on to that pretty smile.

Love you,
Frank

According to the terms of the surrender of September 2, 1945, Japan, unlike Germany, was not divided into zones to be governed by the conquering forces. The American army was to occupy Japan until 1952, at which time the Japanese would resume sole control over their own affairs. Even though the country was to be occupied, Emperor Hirohito was left on the throne as a constitutional monarch and the Japanese parliament retained some of its lawmaking powers. With regard to territory, all lands acquired or seized by Japan since 1875 were taken away.

Thus ended the most destructive war in history. In Europe and the Pacific area combined, more than 400,000 Americans lost their lives, and another 670,000 were wounded. It is estimated that nearly 17 million people lost their lives in the Pacific War. Of this number, more than 13 million were Chinese slaughtered by the Japanese during their invasion of China. If this latter number is close to being accurate, the Chinese theater of the war accounted for more than three-fourths of all deaths in the Pacific during World War II.

Discuss . . .

- possible reasons why the Japanese were so brutal toward the Chinese, who were Asians like themselves.
- whether you feel the surrender terms imposed on the Japanese were too lenient or too harsh. Explain your answer.
- whether you think another world war could take place in the future, and if so, where it might break out.
- why articles labeled "Made in Occupied Japan" have become collectibles.

Answer Key for Activities Involving Further Study or Research

Setting the Stage (page 5)—The United Nations has the power to send troops to a troubled area. The League of Nations had no such power.

The Flying Tigers (page 9)—To exploit the Japanese fear of sharks.

The March of Death (page 13)—The Germans generally treated American POWs better than the Japanese. The Japanese sometimes starved, beat, and executed American prisoners.

The Japanese violated rules of the Geneva Convention by refusing to deliver Red Cross packages and provide adequate food and medicines. They also required Allied officers to work.

The War Under the Sea (page 19)—The *Turtle* looked more like a top than a submarine. It was a one-man boat powered by hand-cranked propellers. Its pilot attempted to plant a bomb in the hull of an enemy ship using a hand-cranked drill.

Island Hopping (page 21)—Solomons–3,000; Gilberts–2,700; Carolines–1,800; Marshalls–2,400; Marianas–600.

The China-Burma-India Theater (page 25)—(1) between India and Tibet (2) India is west of Burma (3) northeast.

Planned Invasion of Japan (page 28)—(1) Hokkaido, Honshu, Kyushu, Shikoku (2) Tokyo; Too many people would have been killed. (3) Honshu; Kyushu; Honshu; War materials and weapons were manufactured in these cities.

The Japanese Steamroller (page 11)

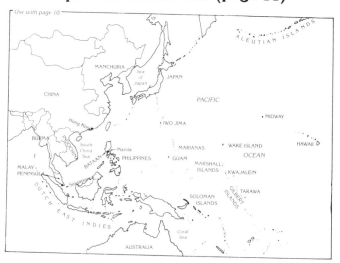

Selected Bibliography

Black, Wallace B., and Jean F. Blashfield. *Iwo Jima and Okinawa*. New York: Crestwood House, 1993.

Harris, Nathaniel. *Spotlight on the Second World War*. East Sussex, England: Wayland Publishers Ltd., 1985

McGowen, Tom. *World War II*. New York: Franklin Watts, 1993.

Nardo, Don. *World War II: The War in the Pacific*. San Diego: Lucent Books, 1991.

Ritchie, Edna. *World War II and the Aftermath*. New York: Golden Press, 1966.

Steinberg, Rafael, and the editors of Time-Life Books. *Island Fighting: World War II*. Alexandria, Virginia: Time-Life Books, 1978.

Wheeler, Keith, and the editors of Time-Life Books. *War Under the Pacific*. World War II. Alexandria, Virginia: Time-Life Books, 1980.

World War II in the Air: The Pacific. Edited by Major James F. Sunderman. New York: Bramhall House, 1962.